Monopillar

Monopillar

Alan Horsfield

Nelson

an International Thomson Publishing company I(T)P®

Melbourne • Albany, NY • Belmont, CA • Bonn • Boston • Cincinnati
Detroit • Johannesburg • London • Madrid • Mexico City • New York
Paris • Singapore • Tokyo • Toronto • Washington

Nelson I T P®
102 Dodds Street
South Melbourne 3205

Email nelsonitp@nelson.com.au
Website http://www.nelsonitp.com

Nelson I T P® *an International Thomson Publishing company*

First published in 1998
10 9 8 7 6 5 4
05 04 03 02 01 00 99
Copyright © Nelson ITP 1999

National Library of Australia
Cataloguing-in-Publication data

Alan Horsfield
    Monopillar
    ISBN 0 17 009432 4
    ISBN 0 17 009414 6 (set).
    I. Title. (Series: BlitzIt).
    A823.3

Editorial production by BDP
Designed by Christine Deering
Illustrations by Grant Adam/Uncommon Characters
Cover designed by Grant Adam/Uncommon Characters
Text designed by Christine Deering
Typeset in Clearface Regular
Printed in Singapore by Kin Keong Printing Co. Pte. Ltd

Nelson Australia Pty Limited ACN 058 280 149 (incorporated in
Victoria) trading as Nelson ITP.

Contents

Science fiction! Sci fi! SF! Whatever you call it! It's all I ever seem to hear about, these days.

Martians...UFOs...the Bermuda Triangle... time travel...close encounters...the Yeti. Little science and all fiction; that's what I think. And how do I know they're all fiction?

It's easy. No one has ever captured a real alien, or a monster; not even on film. If you look closely at the pictures that are supposed to be "evidence", they look so fake it's almost funny. "The truth" caught on film? More like a practical joke. The Loch Ness Monster is a perfect example. Why is it that all of the people who have been lucky enough to see the monster over the years have been such lousy photographers? Fuzzy photos are not evidence!

1

I'm sure no-one has even seen a spaceship, or a Yeti (blurry old footprints don't count), or a water monster, or an alien. But people keep claiming they have. And their reports are all fiction – except for mine, that is.

I'm about to tell you a story that is absolutely true. It will sound like science fiction. It is not. Once you have read this story, and have considered the evidence, you will understand the truth.

Chapter 1

Monorail Mystery

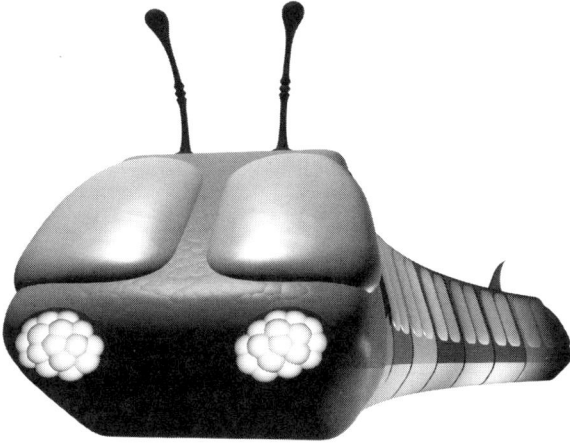

It all started innocently enough. I was on summer holidays, and Mum had been planning a few "educational" activities for me. On this particular day she had decided we should visit the Powerhouse Museum to check out the new electronics exhibition.

We caught a train into Town Hall Station, then boarded one of the monorail trains at Park Plaza. From there we headed towards the old Pyrmont Bridge and the Powerhouse Museum.

Generally, when travelling, I'm more interested in my electronic games than the scenery, but I do like looking at high-tech cars and machinery. I've always liked the monorail. I think it's really interesting, the way the trains travel around above the city on their giant elevated circuit. I like to look out the window at the people and cars below, as small as ants, and at the other trains crawling their way around the circuit like gigantic grubs.

On this trip I'd grown bored with Donkey Kong, so I looked out the window. Our train was sweeping around a curve in the track. There was another train on the track about fifty metres ahead, just rounding the next bend.

As it disappeared around the bend something occurred to me. At a glance, the train ahead of us looked similar to any other train on the monorail. It was long and white, with a coloured stripe down the side of the carriages. There was something wrong,

however. It was *different*.

Somebody else mightn't have noticed, but, as I said, I'd always been interested in the monorail. There was something about the texture of the paintwork and metal that caught my eye. Our train was bright, white and clean, like a new refrigerator, and its polished metal surfaces looked new and shiny. The carriages of the train in front of us were a duller, dirtier, colour that didn't reflect the light. There was something creepy about the texture of the paintwork – it looked a bit like the yellowish-white skin of a living thing.

"Get a grip on yourself!" I thought. "You've been watching a few too many episodes of 'The X Files'!"

As our train rounded the bend and came out on the straight, the train ahead was visible again. I craned my neck to see it, and noticed an antenna sticking up from the top of the last car. As we passed the shadowy wall

5

of the old woolstores, the antenna looked like the erect, short, tail of a wasp. What's more, I caught a glimpse of two wiry antennae on the front that looked like the feelers of an insect.

I knew I was being stupid, but I couldn't help thinking that it was very creepy. I felt a sudden chill run down my spine.

The strange train disappeared around the corner of the Powerhouse Museum. That's where we were getting off. I leaped out before Mum, hoping for a last look at the mysterious train, but it was out of sight. So I took a close look at the train that we had been travelling on. It was bright and shining, with no extra aerials or antennae at the front or the back. Then the doors purred shut and the train hummed off, away from the fluorescently clean, tube-like station.

I was puzzled, but I tried to put it out of my head. Perhaps one of the proper trains

was out of order, and they'd had to put a different model into service for a while. Or maybe my imagination was out of control . . .

Chapter 2

The Three in White

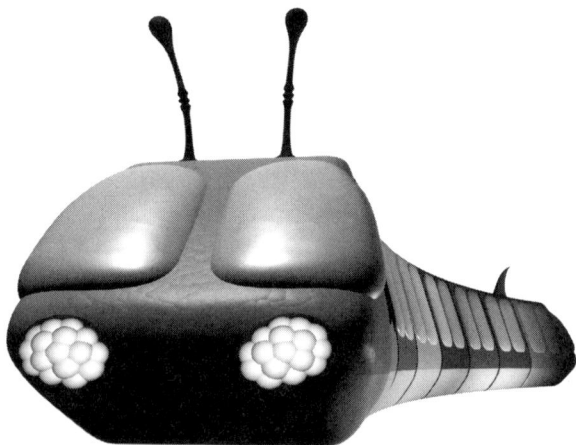

We left the station through the turnstiles, and crossed the long suspended ramp towards the Powerhouse Museum. There were a few other family groups and tourists milling around, obviously heading to the museum, too.

Ahead of us I could see three people in what looked like white lab coats; you know, like doctors wear. They were struggling with a low trolley laden with bulging orange garbage bags. There was a tall, thin woman, and two narrow-eyed men. Normally I wouldn't have paid any attention to them, but there was something secretive, a bit furtive, about them. The men were intent on keeping the bags on the trolley; the woman was walking beside them, snapping orders. She kept looking up and scanning the crowd heading for the museum, and, once, she caught my eye. I looked away immediately. Not before I saw her eyes narrow, however, as if she was trying to commit my face to memory.

"Settle down!" I thought. Strange trains; sinister scientists...it was all a bit over the top.

When we reached the museum, the three in white veered towards a staff-only entrance with their trolley, while we kept moving towards the ticket box.

• • •

I love the Powerhouse Museum. It's the best museum ever; full of high-tech electronics and things called interactive displays – which the

adults take over if you give them half a chance. It's also a great place to explore. There are olden-day suits of armour and modern-day space suits (some things haven't changed very much). Then there are model trains, musical instruments, a Catalina flying boat, and a simply massive Boulton and Watt steam engine. But that stuff's mainly for school projects and class excursions.

The place was once called the Ultimo Power Station, and it was built nearly one hundred years ago to supply electricity for the old-fashioned trams they had in Sydney then. When the trams stopped running the building was empty for close to twenty-five years, before becoming home to the museum.

I'd visited the Powerhouse a couple of times before, on school trips. It was like the past was in the air, filling the building with this spooky feeling. Some kids in my class got a bit scared.

It *can* be kind of eerie if you suddenly find yourself alone in a room, especially one of the dim, dark ones. I don't hang around. You can walk through a doorway and suddenly find yourself in, say, a humming space-shuttle model, ready to take off for deep space. The past and the future: it's all there. No wonder the museum turned out to be the perfect hiding place for…aliens!

• • •

When we entered the museum, I went straight to the computer section while Mum had a look at some old jewellery and ceramics.

Whenever I visited the Powerhouse, I played the noughts-and-crosses machine. I couldn't beat it, but it couldn't beat me either. On about the tenth game I just happened to look up, and saw three people in white having a very intense discussion about fifteen metres away. Beside them was an empty trolley. They were the same three, white-coated scientist-looking people I'd seen struggling across the ramp with the orange garbage bags. Once again, they were trying not to be obvious, but the way they were huddled together meant that I couldn't help noticing them.

Suddenly the woman looked up. A look of recognition crossed her face, and she whispered something urgently to the two men. The three of them glared at me, and I looked away, pretending to examine something on the wall. There was nothing on the wall and I felt a bit stupid. I sneaked another peek at them. They had moved further away, but were still looking at me and whispering to each other.

I felt a bit spooked, and decided to explore some other exhibits. I didn't know what I'd done, but I didn't want to hang around to find out.

Chapter 3

Old Bones

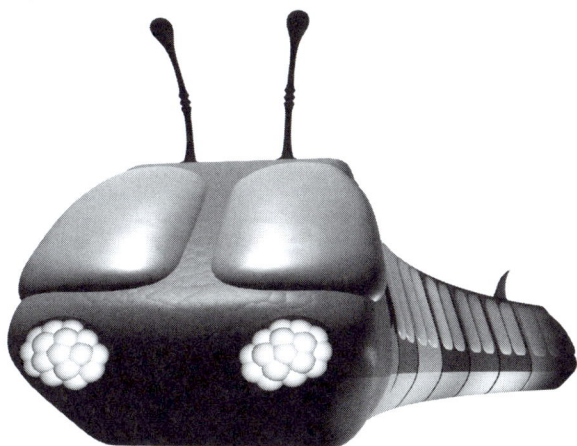

The space shuttle. Another of the fantastic exhibits at the Powerhouse. You can climb into it and get a sense of how astronauts feel when they orbit the earth.

As I climbed up a ladder into the space shuttle I looked over my shoulder – I was feeling a bit nervous by this time. Behind me I caught a glimpse of the three weirdos, with their empty trolley. They were still watching me! What was going on? It was like being followed through a department store by a security guard. Did they think I was planning to steal something, or to vandalise the exhibits? Give me a break!

Then they hurriedly moved on, pushing their squeaking trolley. I decided I didn't like this little band of uniformed oldies being there every time I looked around. I lingered for a while, just to prove to myself I wasn't a coward, then decided it was time to find Mum and tell her I was bored. That would give her an excuse to find something else to do.

I looked for, and found, an EXIT sign to a higher level. I was hoping it would take me to the jewellery exhibits, where I'd find Mum, for sure.

The museum is a maze of levels and walls and ramps and stairways and lifts, and it's easy to get lost, even if you've been there dozens of times. I went left, then right, then straight ahead, trying to find the jewellery and stuff. I must have taken a wrong turn, however, for I found myself in a dim corridor. It was almost hidden behind a collection of large partitions, the sort used to separate the different exhibits.

On one side was a number of doorways bearing signs like: KEEP OUT . . . NO ENTRY . . . STAFF ONLY. One door, carrying a crude, handwritten sign saying TEMPORARY STOREROOM, was ajar. I looked in. I was hoping to find someone who could point me in the right direction.

"Is anyone in there?" I called. There was no answer, so I pushed the door open a crack, and peeked in.

What I saw in there shocked me. The room was full of bones – old bones. I pushed the door open a little further. There were piles of bones all over the place: stacked on shelves, on the floor, on desks and chairs, and in boxes.

"They must be for a new exhibit," I said to myself. But how on earth would the curators put them all together again? I wondered. It would be worse than a 5000-piece jigsaw. And what were the bones from? They looked too small to be dinosaur bones, but then again, they might have been from very small dinosaurs.

I stepped forward and peered into the gloom. Partly hidden in the dark and shadows in the far corner, was what looked like a neat pile of human skulls. A shudder ran down my spine. Then pulled myself together – I remembered that museums often have exhibits of human skeletons along with those of other primates. It had to be a display about evolution and how things change. Still, I didn't like it, or the smell of the place.

Or the fact that on the floor, under the desk, was a bundle of empty, orange, garbage bags.

Suddenly there was a squeaking noise in the corridor. I peered through the partly-open door, my heart in my mouth. It was The Three again, pushing their long, flat, trolley. It was almost as wide as the corridor, and it was loaded with more orange bags.

Something told me that they wouldn't be very happy to see me. I had to escape – and quickly.

Chapter 4

Gulp!

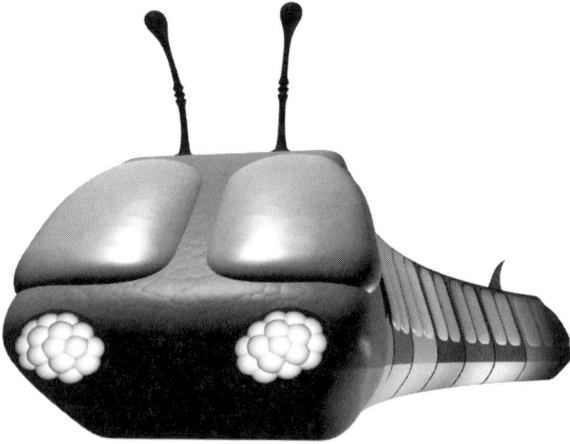

I pelted through the door, down the corridor, around the corner and up another ramp. The Three's angry cries faded behind me. I must have been too quick for them, because they didn't chase me. I ran to the foyer and hid behind a pillar until my heart slowed down.

I found Mum, eventually, in the museum shop. She wandered around for ten minutes, looking at bits and pieces and deciding on postcards for friends overseas. I didn't like the wait. Anything could happen. I had to get her to move ASAP – as soon as possible! I knew what to do ... I had a trick that worked every time.

"Could you buy me a model spaceship?" I asked, innocently.

Mum looked at her watch. "Not right now, Jason. We haven't time. We really should get moving. Next time, maybe," she added kindly.

"Awww, Mum ..." I groaned, just for show. But I was glad to leave.

We followed the suspended walkway back to the monorail station. I was walking so fast that Mum could barely keep up.

Suddenly, I stopped dead. The Three were at the monorail station. They were unloading more bulging orange bags from a stationary train. I resisted going through the turnstile, afraid of something I didn't understand.

Mum looked at me and frowned. I watched, frozen, as The Three entered and exited the darkened train. In their white coats they looked

19

like butchers unloading a meat delivery truck. They were so intent on what they were doing that they hadn't noticed me.

"Come on, Jason. We can't stand here all day watching people working. I have work to do, too."

"There are no lights in that train," I said, holding back. It occurred to me that the interior was, in fact, very dull. Not at all like a typical monorail train. I took a closer look. From the roof of the last car, a single antenna waved stiffly in the breeze. It was the train I had seen earlier!

The Three pulled their squeaking trolley away from the train and out through the Station Manager's gate. I tugged Mum through the turnstile, but they saw us and stopped abruptly to watch. They looked tired and sinister.

By this time the train's interior lights had come on again, but they were still rather dull. Passengers crowded through the doorway, and the doors quickly closed, rather like the mouth

20

of a fish that had just gulped a tasty morsel; not at all like a smoothly operating electronic door. It was very mystifying.

The train filled so quickly there was no room for us. I didn't know it at the time, but we were lucky.

"Now we'll have to wait for the next one," Mum said crossly, giving my arm a sharp tug. "I don't know what's got into you."

I shrugged, but my eyes were on the train. We were close enough to touch it. I almost put my hand out, but I resisted the temptation. Close-up, the body of the train was not smooth and polished like a new car, but more like clean white leather, or like the unblemished skin of some cool amphibian.

The train slid out of the tubular station like an eel emerging from a hole in a river bank. As it slid out of view, it seemed to me that the antennae was moving around as if trying to find a signal; probing the airways, trying to

21

home-in on vital information. It reminded me of an insect with all senses alert, ready for danger – or the next meal.

I looked back through the station entrance to the walkway. The Three were there almost hidden by the curve of the path. They might have been resting after pulling a heavy load, but I had the distinct feeling that they were watching to see whether Mum and I boarded the next train.

We did. It was a brightly-lit train, and looked perfectly normal, but I gave it a good looking-over as it came to a stop.

As the train pulled out onto the long curves of the meandering city circuit, I pulled Donkey Kong out of my backpack. I was trying to put everything that had happened out of my mind. It was just too weird for words.

Chapter 5

Derailed

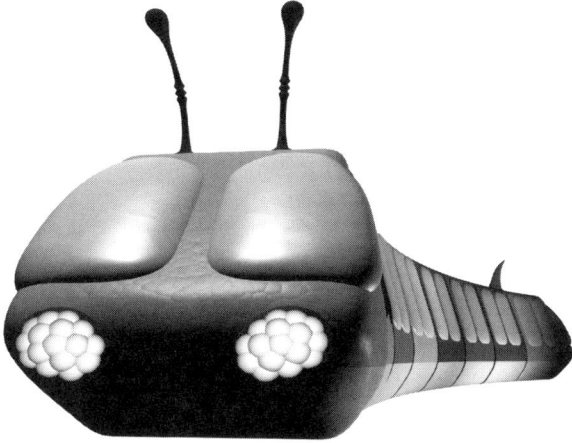

Monorails are amazingly safe. They don't have crashes because they all travel in the same direction around their circuits. They don't run into ordinary trucks and cars because they are well above the roadways and streets. There are no level crossings to deal with. And the monorail track is so strong and wide that it would seem almost impossible for one to fall off.

Mum surprised me a few days later when she said one *had* fallen off. She'd read about it in the paper. It was a big mystery. Apparently the train had moved from the platform at night – all by itself, it seemed – travelled a little way down the track, and then toppled over. It hadn't fallen to the ground; it had actually tipped 180 degrees so that it was now hanging upside-down from the track.

I had to see it for myself. When Mum left for work I ran to the station and caught the next train into the city.

• • •

I found the upturned monorail train just up from the World Square Station. The street had been closed-off to traffic – they were probably afraid that the train might fall onto the road – but pedestrians could sneak through the barriers. Not many people usually used that block, as most of it was taken up with building projects that were progressing very slowly.

A section of road was fenced off with yellow plastic barricades and orange plastic netting. It was not very substantial – more a warning to keep out. The odd thing was that the upturned train did not interfere with the normal running of the other monorail trains. They simply passed overhead on the topside of the rail.

I sauntered down the street and stood on the opposite side of the road to the hanging train. Beneath the train, and inside the fenced-off area, was a mobile crane. Weary workpeople in white protective gear made their way up a temporary ladder to a central door and disappeared inside the train. The carriages must have been attached very securely to the rail, even if they were upside-down.

I looked closely at the train, then felt a shock go through me. It was the same strange train that I had seen on my visit to the museum. It looked different, however. It was duller in colour, and the three strange antennae had shrunk to the size of little bumps.

The centre door opened a little wider and

the workers came out – three of them. I gave a little gasp and stepped back. it was The Three!

Each of them carried four or five large orange bags. They paused at the top of the ladder and surveyed the street. I stepped back into the shadows. They didn't see me, but they certainly took a good look at the other people below.

They struggled down the ladder with their loads, and heaved them into the back of a security van. They were certainly playing safe with their old bones.

The door closed in its odd fish-like way. It was unreal. Then – I swear it really happened! – it shuddered on the track, and made an unearthly noise, like a giant caterpillar burping. It gave me the weirdest feeling. I could almost believe the train was alive! But I knew machines couldn't burp.

Where were all those bones coming from? I wondered. Sometimes, as I was soon to find out, I can be pretty slow!

Chapter 6

Close Encounter

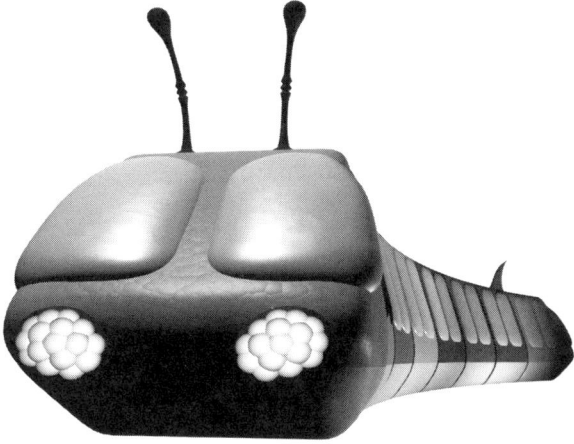

I decided to leave, and headed off up the street to the next block. However my curiosity made me look back at the hanging monster. As I did, the headlights caught my attention. They had lost their bright, glassy, silvery shine. They looked like the unseeing eyes of some dead animal. And the large front windows of the train reminded me of the pretend eyes some insects have to scare off predators.

I lingered too long. The Three, clambering back up the ladder, had seen me. They stopped and watched me watching them. I didn't like it.

I turned the corner, ran for the bus stop, and caught the first bus home.

• • •

But now I was interested. There really *was* something spooky going on. I hadn't imagined it. The Three were using the museum for some sinister purpose, and the strange monorail train was mixed up in it too. It was odd, and I didn't really like it. I particularly didn't like the seemingly endless supply of bones The Three were hiding. Where were the bones coming from?

It was starting to frighten me. But I was also curious. I couldn't help going back again. And I did. The very next day.

• • •

I stopped at the corner and cautiously watched the inverted train from a safe distance. The barricade was still in place, but the ladders had gone. A lone, white-coated security guard patrolled the perimeter of the fenced-off area, which now took up half the street. From a distance the guard looked scrawny and bent-over. Strange. He wasn't at all like the burly guards who usually protect property.

The security guard kept looking nervously up and down the street as if he was expecting problems. There were a few people in the street, but no-one else seemed very interested in the monorail train. Except for me, of course.

The train had changed even more. It was almost the colour of a dull – or dead – goldfish. And it seemed to be rounder and chubbier than it had been the previous day. It looked as if it was sagging towards the ground. Creepiest of all, what looked like a skin had grown over the concertina joins between the carriages.

I snuck down the street, keeping an eye on the security guard, when I noticed that the antennae bumps had almost completely disappeared. I was so fascinated that I stopped, squinting at the train. Wrong move!

"What's your problem, kid?" the guard called from across the street. Then he shouted, "*You* again!"

He was one of The Three! I froze to the spot for a moment. I wanted to hotfoot it out of there but I was too scared.

"Hey, kid! Hey! Come here! You're the kid who's been hanging around!" he squawked as he clambered over the barricade and came after me.

I took off. Behind me I could hear him yelling angrily in his thin, croaky voice, but I knew he wouldn't go too far from his post. I stopped at the corner and looked back. He was hidden behind a few amused pedestrians. My heart was still thumping.

I looked up at the transformed train. Suddenly it shuddered, as if from a momentary spasm. My eyes were playing tricks, I thought.

Probably heat from the road, or haze caused by car exhausts. Without thinking I stepped back towards the barricade.

The train twitched again. A shiver ran down its length. For a moment it was still, then it pulsated briefly.

The guard must have been closer than I realised, for he suddenly ducked from behind a slow-moving glazier's truck, round a couple of people, and made a grab for me.

I yelled, and fled into a nearby Timezone. It was packed out, and I felt safe. He wouldn't try to get me in here. I won six quick tickets on Skill Tester and then rode After Burner – after everything that had happened, I needed some peace and quiet.

Chapter 7

Metamorphosis

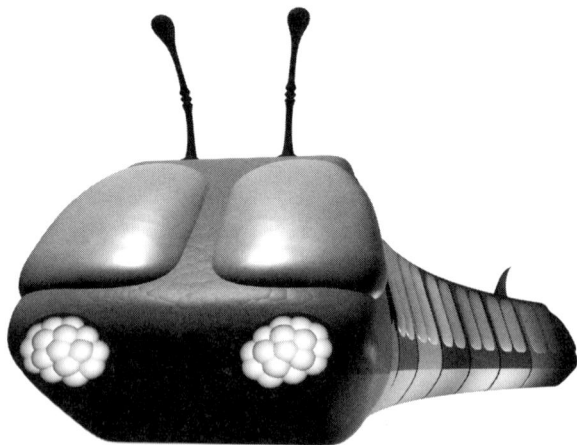

I didn't go back for several days. I wasn't going to go back at all, but a voice in my head kept nagging me, telling me that I needed to understand what was going on. So I returned at dusk, just as the street lights flickered on.

Things had changed. The barricade stretched further along the street. A rectangular construction hut was sitting on the street inside the plastic orange fence. A portable loo was some distance away. KEEP OUT signs faced out in every direction.

I crept up the almost-deserted street and crouched behind a pile of garbage. I wasn't feeling very brave. At least I was in the shadows.

I watched for an hour or so. A monorail train pulled out from the station and hummed up the circuit. It disappeared from sight around the corner of a building.

As it passed the upturned train I compared the two. The passing train was white and bright, with large clean windows and brightly coloured stripes. I could only just make out some of the original markings on the hanging train; they were merely dull patterns on the now-bronze body.

Suddenly the train convulsed with a dull clanging noise. It was then that I realised that whatever *it* was, it wasn't a train any more. It was something else altogether.

The door of the hut flew open. Three people spilled out. The Three again! They waited for a few moments, then the train-thing convulsed again.

The woman shouted some strange commands in a language I didn't recognise. Quickly she and the men pulled another barricade open and stretched it across the street.

The thing convulsed again. A wave of motion ran along its length. More garbled orders were shouted.

Suddenly I realised what The Three had done. They had blocked off both ends of the street – and I was trapped inside their yellow and black barricade.

I looked up. The thing hanging from the rail was almost squirming. I couldn't believe it. More orders were shouted as The Three ran in a frenzy to complete their street barrier. They ran orange plastic netting along the length of each fence, making it impossible for pedestrians to pass through.

It also made it very difficult for me to get out. I had an awful sinking feeling. I was trapped. I didn't dare to move from my garbage heap and it was starting to smell.

The lights in that section of the street snapped off. The rest of the world, just half-a-block away, was bright and noisy. But it was now too dark to make a dash for it.

The Three ran back to their shack, footsteps echoing along the empty street. Another monorail train pulled into the station and pulled out again. It would be the last for the night.

A deep screeching, scraping, sound came from the upturned train. It sounded like it was about to move – *or like it was in pain*. I peered over the litter through the darkness. I could see the bronze body moving as if it were some poor creature trying to escape from a straitjacket. The weak light from the construction hut reflected off the palpitating shape.

The screeching and scraping grew louder.

35

The Three were at the side of their hut, pointing and shouting excitedly. Something was about to happen. Then there was a new sound. It was the sound of tearing … the tearing of metal!

"Look out!" cried the woman. "It's coming!"

What was coming? I wondered. The dull tearing sound continued. I could see the underneath of the train, which was once the roof, splitting open. There was something inside, bursting to get out. *IT* was alive!

A horrible thought swept through me. I knew what IT ate and who made sure IT was fed. Somehow, the train-thing had eaten the passengers who had boarded it. And The Three had removed the bones, and hidden them in the Powerhouse. What a great hiding spot… bones in a museum. They'd have looked like exhibits, rather than evidence.

I grew alert. Suddenly the street was as quiet as a graveyard. I raised my head a little higher from behind the discarded bags of refuse. Something fell from a bag and landed on my face. I gave a little start, then gasped. It was alive, crawling, and it was huge. I squealed and slapped at it. And as I squashed it under the palm of my hand I knew what it was. I could almost feel its final wriggle as it died. I could smell its dirty smell.

I'd mashed a giant cockroach on my face!

Chapter 8

Lift-off!

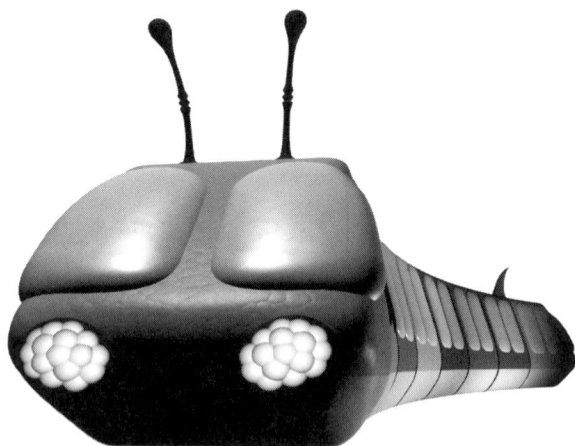

I let out a noise that would have told the whole world I was about to be sick. Without thinking I stood and stumbled forwards trying to wipe the smelly gunk off my face. Then I fell into the bulging garbage bags.

They rattled and burst open as I floundered about, trying to get up. And the more I tried, the more noise I made and the worse things became. More bags burst open and I could feel myself getting wet and squelchy. Strange garbage smells from the torn and burst bags engulfed me.

My stomach heaved.

"Get away," I yelled at the squashed cockroach remains on my face. I tried frantically to wipe the corpse from my face without really touching it. I could feel the warm creamy insides mushed up with the gritty broken shell.

I rolled over, out of the bags and on to the dirty footpath. I was about to call out for help but I was sick first. I had forgotten about The Three. But I had sure let them know that I was there.

After the second heave I heard one call, "It's that interfering kid again. He'll muck everything up."

"Grab the little scum," another called.

I could hear footsteps running in my direction. It was enough to scare me to my senses. I jumped to my feet and began running towards the street lights. Then there was an almighty, tearing, *screech*.

"Forget him," screamed the woman. "He's not worth it." The footsteps hesitated.

"We don't have time!" screeched the woman more urgently. The footsteps stopped, then retreated rapidly.

I stopped too, panting. My breath tasted foul. I looked back. I could see that the train was indeed splitting open to reveal something inside. It was like watching a cicada emerge from its shell. Although this was like no cicada I'd ever seen.

A giant metallic thing emerged, bursting the train shell as if it was cooking foil. Four great robotic arms came out and clutched the monorail track. The bronze cocoon withered up like a discarded skin.

Suddenly, the creature burst into life. Four quietly humming jet-engines slid through panels in the undercarriage. Another panel slid back, and a small ladder glided out towards the street below.

I could see The Three. They hesitated before climbing the ladder. The woman looked around cautiously. Then they all disappeared into the interior. The ladder followed, and the door slid shut.

The engines gave a roar of power and the metallic arms let go of the rail. The machine was suspended above the small hut for a moment. It moved sideways to the centre of the street, hovered for a second or two, then, with a burst of power, blasted off. Real high-tech stuff.

The street turned into a mini-hurricane disaster area. I shut my eyes as dust, grit, garbage bags and paper whipped past my body. As soon as I could, I opened my eyes and looked up. I could just make out the four glowing engines in the starry sky. The sound had faded away.

The street lights burst on, and the four

points of light from the train-thing were suddenly lost in the glare. All that remained was the metallic outer case hanging sadly from the track. I suddenly realised that it was my only evidence. I'd have to get back as soon as I could in the morning to save my proof. There was nothing I could do now, however. I felt as sick as a dog. I needed a bath in a swimming pool, and some food in my belly.

Chapter 9

The Proof

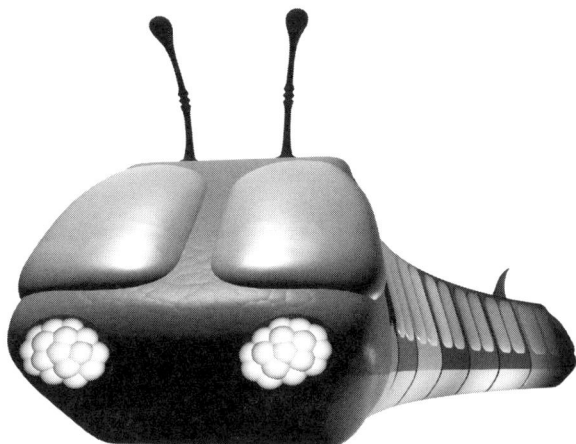

The next morning, before Mum could complain, I went into the city. As soon as I rounded the corner I knew things had changed. The barricades were gone. The little shed and the portable loo were still below the station, but a huge mobile crane was lifting them onto a truck.

And what about the outer skin, the cocoon, my proof? The last I saw of it was on the back of Sam's Scrap Metal truck as it disappeared around the corner. No doubt it was melted down and remade into insect-spray cans. Or something like that.

• • •

All I can say is that every word of this story is true. It is *not* science fiction. The proof was there. You probably saw it yourself without realising it. Everyone's seen a monorail train. And you've all heard stories of people who have disappeared and were never heard of again. Put it all together. Anyone can see the connections. What more proof do you need than that?

About the Author

As a child, **Alan Horsfield's** father told him that if he told a lie, he would get a pimple on his tongue. Being a good child, he listened to his father. Since then, he has never told a lie, not even a little white one. His stories reflect his honesty. When you read *Monopillar*, you will know this for a fact.

Blitz It

Hell-ectric Guitar
by Brian McGinn

Frank meets a mysterious old man who sells him a battered guitar. The guitar can make him a superstar – but what does it, and the old man, want in return? Will Frank last long enough to enjoy his fame?

Birthday Surprise
by Margaret Pearce

Freckles, Frazzle and James think they'll surprise their mother on her birthday with a plant they have grown themselves. The birthday plant however, shows a sinister appetite for food – and worse!

Blitz It

The Twins in the Trunk
by Susan Green

When Katie finds an old trunk in the cellar under her house, she thinks she's found bushranger's treasure. What she *has* found is ghost trouble – and double trouble at that!

Katie and Angus soon find that some things are better left unopened...

Expiry Date
by Raewyn Caisley

Quentin and Andrew think it's pretty funny to tease Richard Corelli. Things go terribly wrong however, and Andrew finds himself haunted by a mysterious stranger. Could Andrew be approaching his "expiry date"?

BlitzIt

BlitzIt is here! Once you've read one *BlitzIt* book, you'll want to read them all.

Mystery ... adventure ... alien visitors ... weird science ... spooky happenings ... *BlitzIt* has something for everyone!

Bargains from Outer Space

by Heather Hammonds

Rod and Sean get more than they bargain for when they flick through the channels on the new TV. Who, or what, are the strange creatures selling fantastic gadgets? And do they really deliver? Find out what happens when Rod and Sean go on a shopping spree that is out-of-this-world!